SandCastle

Let's Go!

LET'S GO
BY
TRAIN

ANDERS HANSON

Consulting Editor, Diane Craig, M.A./Reading Specialist

ABDO Publishing Company

Published by ABDO Publishing Company, 8000 West 78th Street, Edina, MN 55439.

Printed in the United States.

Editor: Pam Price
Curriculum Coordinator: Nancy Tuminelly
Cover and Interior Design and Production: Mighty Media
Photo Credits: Shutterstock

Library of Congress Cataloging-in-Publication Data

Hanson, Anders, 1980-
    Let's go by train / Anders Hanson.
        p. cm. -- (Let's go!)
    ISBN 978-1-59928-903-8
    1. Railroad trains--Juvenile literature. 2. Railroad travel--Juvenile literature. I. Title.

TF148.H325 2008
625.1--dc22

                                                                            2007010190

SandCastle™ Level: Transitional

SandCastle™ books are created by a team of professional educators, reading specialists, and content developers around five essential components—phonemic awareness, phonics, vocabulary, text comprehension, and fluency—to assist young readers as they develop reading skills and increase their general knowledge. All books are written, reviewed, and leveled for guided reading, early intervention reading, and Accelerated Reader® programs for use in shared, guided, and independent reading and writing activities to support a balanced approach to literacy instruction. The SandCastle™ series has four levels that correspond to early literacy development. The levels are provided to help teachers and parents select appropriate books for young readers.

Emerging Readers
(no flags)

Beginning Readers
(1 flag)

Transitional Readers
(2 flags)

Fluent Readers
(3 flags)

SandCastle™ would like to hear from you. Please send us your comments or questions.

sandcastle@abdopublishing.com

Trains run along tracks. They can move a lot of people or heavy goods.

People get on trains at train stations.

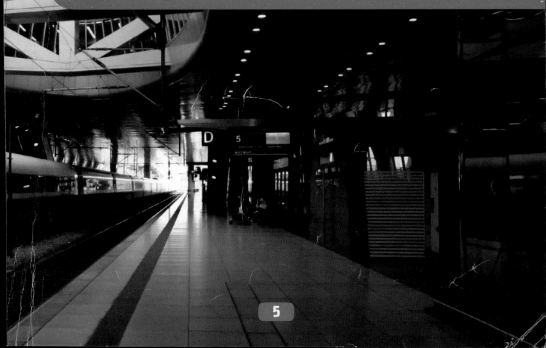

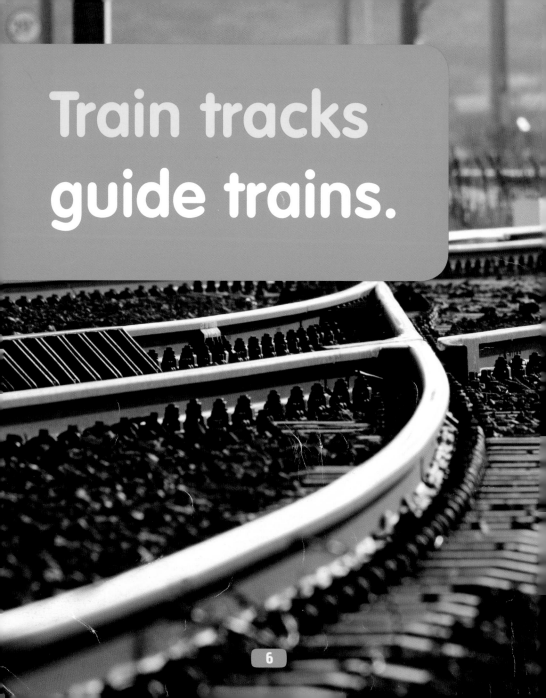

Train tracks guide trains.

Most trains have wheels that rest on the tracks.

Locomotives pull trains.

Sara is ready to
board the train.

13

14

Sasha takes
the train to
visit her uncle.

Tom and his mom
watch the trains
at the station.

18

Kenny loves
to look out
the window.
Things pass by
very quickly.

HAVE YOU BEEN ON A TRAIN?

WHERE DID YOU GO?

TYPES OF
TRAIN CARS

locomotive

railcar

FAST FACTS

Maglev trains use magnets to suspend them in air. They do not touch the track or have wheels. They can go much faster than trains with wheels.

The New York City subway carries about five million people each weekday!

Most trains ride on a track that has two rails. A monorail train rides on a single rail.

GLOSSARY

board – to get on or into a vehicle.

locomotive – an engine that moves on its own power and is used to move railroad cars.

magnet – a piece of metal or stone that attracts iron or steel.

subway – an underground passage for people or trains.

suspend – to support or keep something from falling by using an invisible support.

To see a complete list of SandCastle™ books and other nonfiction titles from ABDO Publishing Company, visit **www.abdopublishing.com**.

8000 West 78th Street, Edina, MN 55439 • 800-800-1312 • 952-831-1632 fax